GLASGOW
Old and New

Jack House

RICHARD DREW PUBLISHING

Glasgow

First published 1974 by EP Publishing Ltd

This edition first published 1983 by
Richard Drew Publishing Ltd
20 Park Circus, Glasgow G3 6BE

ISBN 086267 023 3

Set in Italia Book by John Swain (Glasgow) Ltd
Printed and bound in Great Britain by Butler and Tanner Ltd, Frome, Somerset

Contents

Introduction

There can be hardly any city in the United Kingdom which has changed so completely and so rapidly as Glasgow. Exiled Glaswegians returning to the town on holiday are completely bewildered. Even people who knew Glasgow a few years ago cannot recognise today the scenes which were so familiar to them.

In its heyday Glasgow was the Second City of the Empire and one of the biggest in the world. Now it is the third biggest city in Britain, having had to give way to Birmingham as the second city of this country. According to Sir John Betjeman, Glasgow has the finest Victorian architecture to be found anywhere in the world. British architects, when they held a conference in Glasgow, confirmed this opinion.

But Glasgow District Council decided to turn the place into the City of the 'Eighties. They had to start from scratch, because Glasgow, unlike other big centres in Britain, suffered very little from bombing during World War II. They were obsessed – and I give my own opinion – with the idea that the place should be made safe for the motor car, and this accounts for some of the surprising changes in the city.

In working out this book I have been impressed by several factors. First of all, Glasgow, which remained more or less the same for many years, is now a place where things are either coming down or going up. Scaffolding is everywhere in the centre of the city.

Secondly, and this is perhaps more surprising, Glasgow is much greener than it used to be. There are various suggestions about the origin of the name Glasgow. I could readily provide a dozen, one from the Welsh and the rest from the Gaelic, the tongue spoken by Adam and Eve in the Garden of Eden, which was, as we all know, situated in the Western Isles of Scotland! At any rate, the favourite interpretation of Glasgow from the District Council's point of view is 'dear green place'.

The surprising thing is that this changing city becomes greener day by day. In the following pages you will see that certain scenes have been considerably changed by the growth of trees, plants and shrubs, and it is worth mentioning that Glasgow, with 70 major parks and over two hundred minor ones, has more parks per head of population than any city in Europe.

This book has to a large extent depended on the old prints and photographs which were available. We have collected them from many sources – my own collection of Glasgow pictures, the Mitchell Library and other city libraries, the collection in the Art Department of the Glasgow Herald and the Evening Times, and numerous others.

One of the biggest difficulties in making the book has been to try to take the modern photographs from as nearly as possible the same angle as the original photograph or print. Billy Grandison has performed amazing feats of derring-do and ingenuity in order to achieve this.

This book is intended to evoke Glasgow Old and New. Ever since Will Fyffe first sang, 'I belong to Glasgow, dear old Glasgow town' – a song which has gone right round the world and has even been translated into Russian – people have been particularly interested in this remarkable city; not only Glaswegians, but also visitors who were astonished by what they found in the place.

So this book is a record of a changing city and is as far as I know the only one which shows both the old and the new. How quickly it changes I had not realised myself until I examined the new pictures which were taken to replace those in the 1974 edition. I'm glad to say I have found a big improvement.

Jack House
Glasgow, 1983

George Square   1870

The original centre of the city was Glasgow Cross, but George Square gradually took over. The square was built over a little loch and laid out with gardens, surrounded by hotels, dwelling houses and offices. The statue of Sir Walter Scott is the centre-piece and other statues can be seen, including (left of centre) Queen Victoria, on horseback.

George Square   1983

Some of the statues are still there, but the scene has changed. In the background are the ornate Italian-style City Chambers (being refurbished) and the top of the Cenotaph can be seen above the trees. James Watt is still in the foreground, but Queen Victoria is now behind the Information Bureau on the left. The equestrian statue is of Prince Albert. In the background are the new buildings of the University of Strathclyde.

George Square 1901

The City Chambers is the biggest brick building in Glasgow, although most people do not realise that. The frontage is of stone but the erection behind is of brick. Note the hansom and other cabs and, on the left, the cabmen's shelter, which lasted until 1920.

George Square   1983

The trees have grown in 80 years. The Square is more open.
Buses and cars have replaced the horse-drawn cabs. And the
old gas lamps (now much sought-after by house-owners)
have given way to electric standards.

Queen Street Early 19th century

On the left is the headquarters of the Royal Bank of Scotland. The house formerly belonged to one of the Glasgow Tobacco Lords, William Cunninghame of Lainshaw. On the right, the pillared building is the Theatre Royal, the first theatre in Britain to be illuminated by gas!

Queen Street   1983

William Cunninghame's house still stands on the left, but Corinthian pillars were built at the front when it became the Royal Exchange. The continuation of the building behind the mansion was the hall of the Exchange. The whole is now Stirling's Library. In front stands the statue of the Duke of Wellington by Baron Marocchetti, regarded as the finest statue in Glasgow.

Buchanan Street from St Enoch Square   1906

Horse-drawn traffic prevailed at the beginning of the century.
Only two motor vehicles can readily be seen here — the
private car in the foreground and the Fry's Chocolate van left
of centre in the background.

Buchanan Street from St Enoch Square   1983

Pedestrian precincts have taken over, both in St Enoch Square (immediate foreground) and Buchanan Street. Samuel the jeweller is still at the same corner of Buchanan Street and Argyle Street. The only horses seen in Buchanan Street today are those of the mounted police.

Buchanan Street, looking north   1911

Though tramcars seemed to be everywhere in Glasgow at the start of the century, they were not allowed in Buchanan Street, which was the city's most distinguished shopping centre. Note the boy admiring the up-to-date horseless carriage.

Buchanan Street, looking north   1983
The buildings have hardly changed in the last 70 odd years,
but the street is now a 'dear green place' where people can sit
and stare.

Corner of
Buchanan Street and
Argyle Street   1923
A taxi turns into Buchanan Street just behind
a tramcar which was open back and front on
the upper deck. Note the gentlemen wearing
plus-fours, de rigeur for casual wear in
the 'Twenties.

Corner of
Buchanan Street
and Argyle Street   1983
Taxis cannot turn into Buchanan Street
today because it is a pedestrian precinct!
Burton's building, now regarded (believe it
or not!) as a part of Glasgow's architectural
heritage, has replaced the old shops.

Buchanan Street, looking south   1871

This was the less fashionable end, which only got really posh
below St George's Parish Church, centre background. From
there down to St Enoch's Church, far background, were
clubs, expensive shops and Italian warehouses.

Buchanan Street, looking south   1983

After more than 110 years there have been few changes in the buildings on the right-hand side. The Waverley Temperance Hotel is now the Buchanan (licensed) Hotel, beside the Buchanan Street Subway Station. The Royal Scottish Academy of Music and Drama has replaced the tenements between the hotel and the kirk, and the Stock Exchange has been built on the other side. St Enoch's Church has disappeared.

St Vincent Place   1912

St Vincent Place saw plenty of tramcars (better known as 'the caurs') for it was a switching area as well as having through lines. The buildings on the left are the Clydesdale Bank, the 'Citizen' office, the Anchor Line office and the Bank of Scotland.

St Vincent Place   1983

St Vincent Place looks much the same as it did in 1912, even
to the public lavatory. The Clydesdale Bank is still on the left,
but the other offices are in different hands. In the foreground
is the entrance to the Buchanan Street pedestrian precinct.

George Street 1922

George Street was a respectable residential area but by the time this picture was taken it was going down in the world. The tall building on the right of the picture was owned by a cigarette-making firm. Behind the church spire can be seen one of the domes of the City Chambers.

George Street   1983

The last of the old tenements are seen on the left – the cigarette building now belongs to the University of Strathclyde. The church has gone and is replaced by trees, but the dome of the City Chambers can still be seen. The modern building on the right of the street is also a part of the University of Strathclyde.

Gordon Street   1911

Gordon Street was the first sight of Glasgow for many a visitor who arrived at Central Station (right). In the good old summertime men wore straw hats, as you can see, and awnings protected shop windows from the glare. The 'Greek' Thomson building on the left was the famous Grosvenor Restaurant.

Gordon Street 1983

Architecturally, Gordon Street has not changed one whit in 70 years. A traffic policeman is now unnecessary. The Grosvenor is now an office block. Behind the hoardings on the right changes are being made to the entrance to Central Station.

Union Street, looking north   1914

Rush-hour in Glasgow. As you can see by the clock it is 5 p.m., and the workers of the world, and shopping housewives, are making for trams to take them home to the suburbs. The man standing in the way of the Springburn tram (foregound) is not courting death. He is a tramway employee who keeps tram crossings free from grit.

Union Street, looking north   1983

Boots' store now dominates the scene. Their clock shows
11 a.m. and there is little rush. The tramlines have gone.
Many of the buildings, notably on the extreme right and left,
are new.

West Nile Street   1930

A familiar sight in West Nile Street until World War II was the line of trace-horses waiting to help horse-drawn lorries up the steep incline to the north. The figures in the doorway on the right are trace-boys awaiting a job. The Clydesdale horses were owned by Wordie and Company and won many prizes at shows.

West Nile Street   1983

You'll hardly see a horse in the centre of Glasgow nowadays, though there are still plenty on the perimeter. There are new buildings on the left of the street. But farther down the scene is unchanged, with the Charles Rennie Mackintosh tower of the former 'Glasgow Herald and Evening Times' building in the background.

Morrison's Court, Argyle Street   1931

Morrison's Court is one of the oldest parts of Argyle Street and it was here that John Morrison built his eating house. 'Arcade Cafe' signifies the old entrance, changed to the back door when the new entrance was made in the Argyll Arcade, opened in 1828.

Morrison's Court, Argyle Street   1983

The scene has hardly changed in over 50 years, except that there is no horse in the background and the cars are different. The cobbles look unchanged, but the present owners of the restaurant have brightened up the frontage. It is the oldest restaurant in Glasgow.

St Enoch Square   1929

Ironically, this picture was taken to show the St Enoch Subway Station, proposed for demolition to widen the bottleneck into Argyle Street and Buchanan Street. The station is now regarded as a piece of Late Victorian architecture worth preserving. Also ironically, this picture was taken from St Enoch Station, which has been demolished.

St Enoch Square 1983

So far from opening the bottleneck, the authorities have now completely closed it to through traffic, and shrubs and trees have been planted. From St Enoch Square public transport in the form of stalwart Highlanders once carried ladies to various parts of Glasgow in sedan chairs.

Trongate 1914

One of the eight streets of Glasgow which Daniel Defoe saw in the 18th century, the Trongate has two venerable buildings – on the right the steeple of Tron St Mary's Church and in the distance, left of centre, the Tolbooth Steeple, built in 1626. Note the open-upper-deck tramcar and the line of billboard men on the right.

Trongate 1983

Architecturally, the scene has not changed much in 70 years.
The dome which marked the former Glasgow Cross railway
station has disappeared, but the mounted statue of William
of Orange, which was by it, is now in Cathedral Square.

Trongate, looking west   1901

This view is interesting from the sartorial point of view. A typical Glasgow 'shawlie' is seen in the right foreground. On the left is Glasgow Cross station, and just above the heads of the passengers on the Ibrox tram you can see King Billy on his horse. He is portrayed as a Roman Emperor.

Trongate, looking west   1983
Glasgow Cross railway station has gone. Buses run instead of tramcars. The buildings, including the steeple of Tron St Mary's, are substantially unaltered, but the Tron Church has become the Tron Theatre Club.

The Bridgegate, looking towards Saltmarket circa 1870

The Bridgegate was once a fashionable street which went down in the world. Obviously the inhabitants did not take kindly to photographers. This is where many of the Irish immigrants settled when they left their native isle during the 'Hungry 'Forties'.

The Bridgegate, looking towards Saltmarket   1983

A railway bridge has been built over the Bridgegate and some of the old tenements are being preserved. On the right is Shipbank Lane and the people entering it are going to shop in 'Paddy's Market', which has a direct relationship with the poor Irish who made the Briggait their centre.

Richmond Street   1930

When well-to-do Glaswegians left the Glasgow Cross area for better housing, many of them settled in Richmond Street and in adjacent thoroughfares. Note the pillared entrance to the house on the right. Cobbled streets existed in Glasgow until a few years ago, and occasionally a bit of one may still be seen.

Richmond Street   1983
The modern buildings of the University of Strathclyde have replaced the modest terrace, and students stroll where city merchants and shopkeepers once walked.

East Clyde Street, looking west   1914

A morning scene outside the Glasgow Fish Market, on the right. The picture was taken from under the Glasgow and South Western Railway bridge across the Clyde, leading into St Enoch Station. Tramcars are crossing Victoria Bridge. Apart from them, the traffic is almost entirely horse-drawn.

Clyde Street, looking west   1983

'East' has long been dropped from the street's name. The
Fish Market is to be developed as a communal centre. Trees
hide Victoria Bridge. And the railway bridge no longer carries
trains into St Enoch Station, which is to be developed too.

Clyde Street   circa 1820

Joseph Swan, who made this engraving, cheated a bit in this view of the north bank of the Clyde. It shows on the right the Town Hospital and Poorhouse, built in 1733. In the centre stands the new Catholic Chapel, completed in 1817. The horses and carts in the foreground show how shallow the river could be at this point.

Clyde Street   1983

The camera shows a more realistic view across the Clyde. The only building which remains is the Catholic Chapel, now St Andrew's Cathedral. Warehouses stand on either side and in front is the new river walkway. On the right is the sailing ship 'Carrick', now the RNVR Club. The river is deeper and is occasionally dredged.

Bridge Street Station   1939

This was the original main railway station in Glasgow and stood on the south side of the River Clyde not far from Jamaica Street Bridge. It was superseded when Central Station was built on the north side of the river. When this picture was taken, the pillared entrance and adjoining buildings were all that was left of the station.

Site of Bridge Street Station   1983
The station entrance has been demolished (despite pleas
from railway enthusiasts). In the background is the bridge
which carries the railway over the Clyde to Central Station.

Corner of Broomielaw and Jamaica Street   1914

Paisley's Corner was famous in Glasgow for well over 100 years. A single motor car moves grimly through the horse traffic and a tramcar in Jamaica Street waits for a chance to cross. On the left is the railway into Central Station and the hoardings show that holidays in Nice and Monte Carlo were being offered to Glaswegians in 1914.

Corner of Broomielaw and Jamaica Street   1983

Although it looks considerably brighter, the corner has changed very little in 70 years, though it is no longer Paisley's, which has removed to the other side of Jamaica Street. Architecturally it remains the same group of buildings — they now belong to Sir Hugh Fraser, whose monogram appears on the sunblinds. Signs of electrification can be seen on the railway into Central Station.

The Broomielaw, looking west   1920

When this picture was taken the Broomielaw was the place from which the Firth of Clyde sailings took place. Ships from England, Ireland and farther afield discharged goods here, as can be seen from the variety of lorries. The River Clyde is behind the buildings on the left.

The Broomielaw, looking west   1983

Ships and steamers no longer come as far up the Clyde as the Broomielaw, owing to the new Kingston Bridge (left background). Many buildings on the right-hand side have been demolished and replaced. The only remaining nautical touch is the frontage of the restaurant below the whisky sign. The Clyde walkway is now being developed.

Glasgow Harbour   1895

Ships of all kinds thronged into the River Clyde at Glasgow in Victorian times. As much traffic and goods came in by river as by rail. Farther down the river were the famous Clyde shipyards, where the shipbuilders claimed to turn out the biggest and best ships in the world.

Glasgow Harbour   1983

The only shipping now seen in the upper reaches of Glasgow Harbour are dredgers and police launches. In the background is the Kingston Bridge, which has considerably altered cross-river traffic.

THE CLYDE, GLASGOW FROM SAILORS HOME.

The Clyde from Sailors' Home, Broomielaw   1900

Passenger steamers comprise most of the shipping at the Broomielaw side and at the Bridge Wharf opposite. They took a multitude of people 'doon the watter' every summer.

The nearest railway bridges take trains into Central Station on the left. Other Clyde bridges can be seen in the background.

The Clyde from Sailors' Home 1983

It was not possible to take this picture from the same angle as the one on the previous page, but the river can be seen to be empty. The building with the dome on the left is the headquarters of the Clyde Port Authority. In front of Central Station railway bridge is the George V Bridge for motor and pedestrian traffic. A river walkway now takes the place of the old sheds.

Glassford Street   1828

Joseph Swan did this engraving especially to show the Trades House of Glasgow, the building on the right with the dome. It is an Adam building and the only one in Glasgow still used for its original purpose, the meeting of the Incorporations of Trades of the city. As you can see, they were digging up streets even then!

Glassford Street   1983

Nearly 155 years later the Trades House is the only building still in existence. On the extreme right are the headquarters of the Savings Bank of Glasgow. Warehouses now run down both sides of Glassford Street, but here and there some century-old buildings are still in use.

Ingram Street, looking west   1828

John Knox, a distinguished Glasgow artist, made this drawing soon after the rebuilding of the Ramshorn Kirk on the right. The street has been widened, as can be seen by the demolition of a protruding house on the extreme right. The tower of Hutchesons' Hospital is in the centre, and at the end of the street is the Tobacco Lord's mansion which is now part of Stirling's Library

Ingram Street, looking west   1983

You can see why Glasgow is known as 'the dear green place' when you look at the growth of the trees round the Ramshorn Kirk. New warehouses have got into the way of the view of the Hutchesons' Hospital tower. The Corinthian pillars and clock tower of Stirling's Library replace the view of the Tobacco Lord's House.

Glasgow from the Fir Park   1828

The Fir Park became the Necropolis in 1832, but it was a pleasant place of resort in 1828. On the right is the Cathedral, and a funeral is taking place in the kirkyard. This engraving shows the western clock tower and consistory house, both of which were later removed.

Glasgow from the Necropolis   1983

As nearly as possible this photograph shows the scene from the same point as the artist's. The oldest house in Glasgow (Provand's Lordship, 15th century) can be seen peeping round a tree to the left on the far side of the street. The buildings in the background are those of the University of Strathclyde.

39784 Glasgow Necropolis. F.F.& Co.

The Necropolis   1901

The Necropolis, standing beside Glasgow Cathedral, is the burying ground of the Merchants' House of Glasgow and was opened in 1832. The vaults in the foreground are actually within the Cathedral confines. The statue on the hill is of John Knox, the Reformer. His expression as he looks over the city is severe.

The Necropolis   1983

Once again here is evidence that Glasgow is the 'dear green place'. Foliage almost obliterates the view, though John Knox looks grimmer than ever. The object in the left foreground is a mort-safe, used to prevent body-snatchers from stealing coffins and corpses.

Sauchiehall Street   1954

Taken from the roof of La Scala Cinema, this picture shows Sauchiehall Street when tramcars were beginning to lose their ascendancy – though not in this street apparently. The building in the right background was the new NAAFI: that on the left was Green's Playhouse, once the biggest cinema in Europe.

Sauchiehall Street   1983

Thirty years later and Sauchiehall Street is dwarfed by a new high-rise office block where the YMCA used to be. The NAAFI is now the headquarters of the Reo Stakis organisation, with high-rise flats on the skyline; and where the tramcars ran is now a pedestrian precinct.

39763. Glasgow. Sauchiehall Street F.F&C°.

Sauchiehall Street   1900

Though it achieved worldwide fame as a shopping centre and fashionable thoroughfare, Sauchiehall Street was a late starter and, although this picture shows some imposing warehouses and other buildings. there were still mansion houses with gardens just over the hill. It was the way to the West End and so became an exclusive street until Buchanan Street bested it.

Sauchiehall Street   1983
This part is now a pedestrian precinct. Glasgow's best stores,
Copland and Lye's and Pettigrew and Stephen's have been
replaced by the Sauchiehall Street Centre, but a number of
the buildings are the same as 83 years ago.

Sauchiehall Street, west end   1900

At the west end there were still in 1900 private houses with their own gardens. From them were views to Kelvin Park. The tower of the Theological College can be seen in the right background. Sauchiehall Street was at this end mainly residential.

Sauchiehall Street, west end   1983

The place has changed so much that it is difficult to orientate
oneself. But there are clues in the tenements, bottom left,
and in the church spire. Everywhere new buildings have
gone up

Charing Cross 1901

Charing Cross Mansions have obliterated the old Albany
Place, but are still dominated by the Grand Hotel, which was
regarded as the most fashionable in Glasgow. The Charing
Cross fountain worked in those days!

Charing Cross   1983

The changes are readily identified because the fountain on the left and Charing Cross Mansions, centre right, are obvious pinpoints. Over the years the fountain has, owing to subsidence caused by traffic, tilted to one side and is now known as Glasgow's equivalent to the Leaning Tower of Pisa!

39757 Glasgow Kelvingrove Park. F.F. & Co.

Kelvingrove Park   1870

The scene of the great Glasgow Exhibitions of 1888, 1901
and 1911. The building to the right of the Stewart Fountain is
the first Kelvingrove Museum, behind which lies the western
end of Sauchiehall Street.

Kelvingrove Park   1983

Another case of the 'dear green place' affecting the view. The statue of the tigress and the fountain, and the distant view of Sauchiehall Street, are all that we can still see. The tigress was given to Glasgow by an American Glaswegian and a replica stands in Central Park, New York.

Woodside Place   1901

Coming up from Sauchiehall Street in the old days you saw the tall tower of the Theological College, with its attendant towers to the east, and the opposing tower of Park Church on the left. The story goes that one religious body tried to outdo the other. Everything is trim and quiet.

Woodside Place   1983
Trees are taking over yet again. So are motor cars. The dear
quiet place has however become a dear busy place. Park
Church Tower can be seen behind trees, which is maybe just
as well because the tower is all that remains of the church.

Hyndland   circa 1900

Suburbia, not even quite close suburbia, is seldom commemorated. Here is a view, taken at the turn of the century, of the area which is now Hyndland. On the high ground to the left is Gartnavel Mental Hospital, then a bright and shining new building. On the right is Hyndland Church, with Hyndland railway station near by.

Hyndland   1983

This scene has been photographed from approximately the same position as the old one. New terraces have blotted out the pastoral aspect and even the former landmarks. The only point of contact is the roof of Hyndland Church, which can be seen peeping over the rooftops to the left of the other church tower. It's a moot point whether the view is better or not!

Great Western Road, Anniesland circa 1935

Reasons for pictures are often as interesting as the pictures themselves. This was taken to show the 'bottleneck' at Anniesland on the Great Western Road. It was proposed to eliminate it at a cost of £37,000. The bridge leads to a railway station on the right.

Great Western Road, Anniesland   1983

The road has been widened but otherwise things look much
the same. A cinema has been built where there was once
only waste ground: it is now a bingo hall. The railway bridge
is better. And there are more trees.

Castlebank Street, Partick   1890

Partick was an old village when Glasgow was still growing up. These thatched buildings, one of them crow-stepped, belong to old Partick. 'New' tenements have been built uncomfortably alongside them. Castlebank Street takes its name after the Bishop's Castle on the banks of the River Kelvin, to which he repaired on holiday.

Castlebank Street, Partick   1983

The tenements have disappeared. Buildings have been swept away to give access to the expressway which runs along the side of the River Clyde to the left. The cranes of shipbuilding yards can be seen in the background, but whether or not they are in use is another matter.

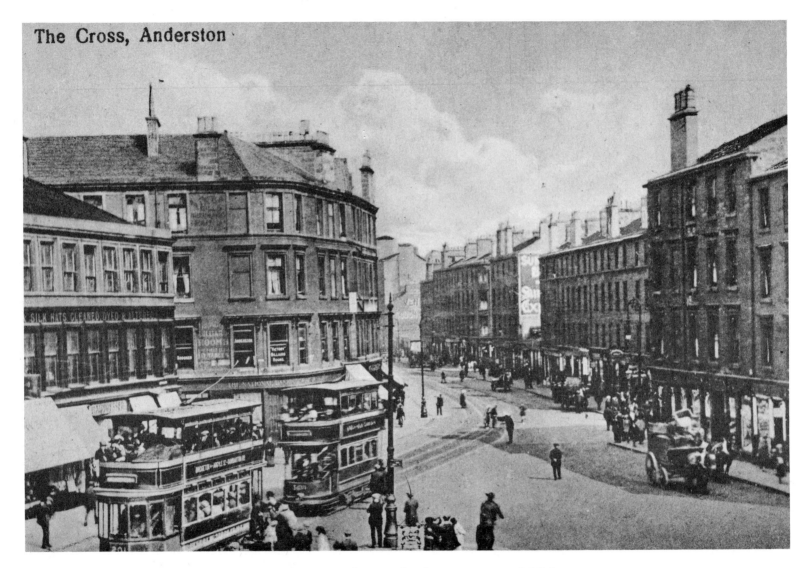

Anderston Cross, looking east   1920

The village of Anderston was once a weaving place outside Glasgow. There was, until recent years, a boundary stone on the right-hand side of Argyle Street (seen here) which marked the entry into Anderston from Glasgow. The area looking reasonably prosperous here, went down as the years passed.

Anderston Cross, looking east   1983

This, believe it or not, is the same scene, taken from the same angle. There was a railway station at Anderston Cross and in the foreground you can still see the platform in a tunnel. This is now one of Glasgow's 'spaghetti junctions'. Among the new buildings is Glasgow's Holiday Inn.

Paisley Road Toll   1890

The ubiquitous horse of Victorian days is again in evidence.
The equipage (right centre) belongs to a wellknown doctor
in the district.

Paisley Road Toll   1983

There have been few architectural changes. The tenements in the background are the same, though the shops have been brightened up. The carriage-hirer's building is essentially the same, but has been tarted up to become the Grand Ole Opry Club.

EAST SIDE OF WATER ROW, GOVAN. 24TH MAY 1861.

Water Row, Govan   1861

Water Row led from Govan Cross down to the River Clyde, and it must be remembered that Govan kept itself clear from Glasgow for many years. Even today Govanites regard themselves as quite different from Glaswegians. The tavern seen here was a regular port of call for travellers who were going to board the steamers at Govan Pier.

Water Row, Govan   1983
From the ornamental fountain at Govan Cross we look on
what remains of Water Row. There are no old houses left.
Even the famous Govan Ferry, which carried people and
vehicles across the river. has gone.

Govan Parish Church Kirkyard   1920

Govan Parish Church is on the site of a Druids' Temple, and in the grounds and the church are some of the finest examples of burial memorials to be found in Britain. In some cases there are stones with heathen inscriptions on one side and Christian on the other. The tombstones in this picture are more recent. In the background is the Pearce Institute.

Govan Parish Church Kirkyard   1983

Little seems to have changed in the last 60 or so years but, if you look carefully, you can see what weather and vandals can do in the way of destruction. Of the tallest memorial only the plinth is left, and all that remains of the strong railings in the central tomb are the posts.

Battle of Langside Memorial   1888

Mary Queen of Scots was defeated by the Regent Moray at
the Battle of Langside in 1568. This monument was erected
at the top of the hill where her generals finally gave in.

Battle of Langside Memorial   1983

Langside has grown from a village to an important Glasgow suburb since the Battle Memorial was erected. The crossing is now an important road junction and there is a fine church opposite the Memorial.

Old Cathcart 1870

Cathcart was an old village outside Glasgow, but it is now within the city boundaries. Up the road in this picture is the Court Knowe, across from Cathcart Castle, where Mary Queen of Scots stood and watched her army being defeated. The road to the right takes you to an ancient bridge and the old Cathcart Snuff Mill.

Old Cathcart   1983

Cathcart is one of the pleasantest of Glasgow suburbs (although true Cathcart supporters still think of it as a place apart) and has a fine park attached to it. Here and there efforts have been made to preserve the old buildings. Careful examination will show that the buildings on the left are part of the old cottages in the facing picture.

Crossmyloof Row, Strathbungo   Mid-Victorian

Strathbungo (over whose name arguments still rage) was a village on its own but, like so many others, it was taken over by Glasgow. This row of cottages stood just opposite Crossmyloof railway station. The board advertising the station is on the right.

Moray Place, Strathbungo 1983

The famous Glasgow architect 'Greek' Thomson came to Strathbungo and transformed Crossmyloof Row into elegant terraces. This shows the start of a fine series of houses. The remains of Crossmyloof station are still on the right, but it ceased to operate many years ago. Strathbungo is now regarded as a preservation area.

Index